Once the Earth had Two Moons

D. Walsh Gilbert

Cerasus Poetry
London N22 6LY

cerasuspoetry.com

for my daughters

in memory of my mother

Contents

"Well, women with breast cancer are warriors..."

—Audre Lorde, *The Cancer Journals*

Discovery

My home & garden sprawl atop the canopy
of a single tree so tall some stars blink beneath it.

When it rains, I collect buckets of sweet rainwater
in a curved magnolia leaf

and dribble raindrops onto dahlia and lily.
Droplets jewel my ears. My two kittens play in puddles.

It's my story to tell,
though some may not believe it.

My birdhouse floats as if suspended by balloons,
my fledgling mouth at the portal of tomorrow.

I ask the poppies who don't know,
What rare bird shed the feathers hanging in the undergrowth?

I nest singing like a wood thrush atop a tufted peony,
rosebuds close behind my shoulder,

and run fingers over my décolletage. I'll feel
the gall inside my petal breast at dawn—

hard as a celestial marble.

The First Appointment

My rowboat lies on a deep-lake surface
while clouds gather underwater—
my world is upside-down.
Doctors hover.
They sky-fish with a birdcage on a string.

The cage door opens.
Blackbirds flock. Wings spread.
Count them: one, five, nine.

Get a net.
Get an ax.
Birds roost on a deadly branch
which leans against my living tree.

I can't see the rotten lumber,
where it's planted,
how it grows,
or how it feeds the crows.
But, it scratches on my keel
and threatens capsize.

Waiting for Test Results

Who strung this tightrope
between the spires of two minarets?
I dance along it with a vampire.
His bat wings balance us—
me in my apron tied in the back,
faking a smile.
It's so far down.

Take another step, he says,
backwards. Let me lead.
Fir trees silhouette, point their needles high.
We scrape our heads on the sky's dark matter.
It's so far down.

The moon is shining. He can last
all night, my vampire,
in his top hat and tails, daring to stand
on one leg while I cling to his neck.
I shield my own with a tilt of my chin
and listen for the minaret's call to prayer.
It must be nearly morning.

Remember Mamma's Trials

Her first escape attempt:
she tied a rosary leash
of saltwater pearls to a purple hummingbird,
but the stone within her breast
had swelled too heavy,
and oak roots had sown in the pit of her belly.

She wrapped her arms around a wolf—
even he had less growl
and blunter teeth
than the host of gnawing termites
burrowed in her feathers.

She grew a rack of antlers,
unsure whether she was hunter or the hunted,
and drank the doctor's brew
of toad and salamander.

But night dropped,
and while lightning bugs
tiptoed on the summer yarrow,
blinked, and disappeared
inside that yellow devil's nettle,

she whispered to the wolf,
Sweet dreams,
traced the cross
of the constellation Cygnus,
and lodged among the falling stars.

Hospital Intake Consultation

Vowels and consonants rain
onto my black umbrella—
bounce and patter in nonsense syllables.

They could spell *malignant,* or
maybe it's *malformed.* My ears scramble
know into *no.* Garbled letters hum,

trying to reassemble into words
from a rainfall alphabet
—a baffling, alien lullaby.

They pile like leaf litter.
It's no use. It's time
to undergo, and no

layer-on-layer of yoke lace
ruffled on my bodice can hide me. Good-bye.
Letters drizzle. They fade and overlap

as sounds tumble—disjointed Courier
voices in the background—
my own cursive font caught in my throat.

Surgery

I am a damsel fly,
teal green,
transparent,
bathed in light,
as delicate as pink
hydrangea
in an acid fog.

My two veined wings
are pinned wide
on a cotton sheet.

A man in a bowler hat
readies
for business,
stiletto hidden
behind his back,

ready
for metamorphosis,
ready
to dig into the dust
of my globe
for his specimen.

His bowler is a bucket.
My world falls into it.

Sleeping in Recovery

I dress my hair with marigolds and violets.
Intoxicated, I ride a chestnut stallion,
side-saddle, and leap him through a flaming hoop.
No reins against the soft of his mouth.
My crop's unnecessary. He must know the way.

My eye's a telescope of new perspective,
and for a time, ferns squeak as they unfurl.
A kaleidoscope of toucans chatters—I can
keenly see the voices of a cockatoo and parrot.
My ear bone hollows into a flute and celebrates.

I scribble *Allons-y* onto a parchment map
and mount a hot air balloon which carries me
smoothly in its dainty teacup basket.
I sip Earl Grey. I'm a vintage English lady
reading fables, full-bosom exposed:

> *Alice had not a moment to think*
> *about stopping herself before*
> *she found herself falling down*
> *what seemed to be a very deep well.*

Until, as gently as the waning crescent moon
cradles its unseen missing half,
the memory of ice skates, diapers, plastic Breyer
horses, and my toddlers' puckish toes,
calls me back.

Message in the Dream

Urgent instructions behind moving clouds insist,

> *Force yourself to pass every roadkill*
> *on your morning walk just to make sure*
> *it's not you.*

> *But, savor the bachelor buttons, purslane,*
> *and the Queen Anne's lace on the highway verge*
> *in the gravel.*

> *Believe: birds break from your skull when you're*
> *not looking—they return with riches*
> *as you sleep.*

I hear the echoes in the message:
> *It's not you*
> *in the gravel*
> *as you sleep.*

First, I'll wash my hair in the wet ether, and let
minnows mix with my curls.
They'll feel like butterflies escaping their cocoons.

My hive has called, and everyone needs to come home
to a teapot pouring bumblebees.
That's how the honey's made. Later,

adventures will beckon again. For now, I've learned
how to trap moonlight in a streetlamp,
how to listen to the blinks of lightning bugs in bushes.

They get brighter when the night grows darker.
That's when owls draw maps with their wings
and walking sticks become magic wands.

Pain:

Scalpels razor unscarred skin:
    the burn
Pectorals rip from collar bone and rib:
    the opened cage
Eyes ink a naked body; men judge inside:
    woman laid bare
Blood salts the knotted suture lines:
    play Cat's Cradle
    plait the Jacob's Ladder

All the magician's fingers:
    abracadabra
        et Voila!

*

Left on an ombré rooftop, she rocks the blue world nestled in her lap
and wishes on the Pleiades:
    Seven Sisters, save me.

Then, a masked man with a watering can
Trickles spider venom straight into her heart:
      Cytophosphane, Methotrexate, 5-Fluorouracil

Until, more babies can curl only in the cavity of her mind,
boughs axed off the lullaby tree:
    barren secrets

Now, this Empress will crown her unnamed, unborn grandchildren
with broken window glass:
    invisible stars in the dark

*

Fully woken to the clink of scissors in the stainless-steel bowl
    labelled
    Biohazard Crematorium:
    Waste.

The Bedside Nurse

The howl of monstrous silence at midnight.
A woman delivers a silver tray
of clouds cushioning the moon's last phase

like a slice of honeydew on whipped cream.
She opens me whole—a folded paper-doll
cut so neatly along a lead-pencil outline.

She's used to finding missing things
such as absent appetites, empty wombs,
the stories the furiously mad repeat:

> Hallucinations of harlequin cats
> in polka-dot ruffles & pom-pom hats
> balanced on a topiary in a terracotta pot.

She knows none of this is real.

White feathers fall like self-forgiveness.
I say, *I love your skirt*—a wedding dress
white-drifting like quiet feathers of a dove.

They scatter as she walks, feathers loosed
in garden undergrowth. Goose down. Seraphim.
I'd recognize an archangel anywhere.

Voices of Visitors

So young...

Did you nurse the girls too long?
Did you feed them toxic milk?

Once the Earth had two moons, too.

Twiggy is flat and people love her.

I told everyone you're on a cruise.
They wondered where you went.

Does it hurt?

Here you are, Queen of the Castle
in your private room.

Don't ever hold a cat. You'll pop.

Reconstruction: like changing tires on a truck.

You know that she can hear you...

Bound for Home

Through air sweeter than the surrounding world,
I descend genuinely opalescent. My parachute,
made of daisies, billows—vanilla, lemon, cantaloupe.

My arms raise to grasp a multitude
of guy-lines. And even as my old body
disintegrates into butterflies and moths,
I stabilize. Once I rode a horse
made of stationary foliage.
Now I float:

> *Either the well was very deep,*
> *or she fell very slowly,*
> *for she had plenty of time*
> *as she went down to look about her,*
> *and to wonder*
> *what was going to happen next.*

Bandages

Once upon a time, the dress fit
the way a key unlocks a treasure chest.

Inside lay emeralds, pearls, and maps
to hidden places.

With my shoulder slipped from my blouse,
I could reach to the bottom and withdraw jewels

to enlighten me. I could gaze at goldfish
in an eggcup and see beauty.

I could glance into a pool
and a pink waterlily would look back at me.

But gauze is not a silk or velvet corset,
and it wraps until la danse du ventre stills.

Behind the curtains, I expect
the mystery to be solved. I could use

a microscope to see my new gown's tiny stitches,
but I can't bear to look.

Artificial Implant

The painting on the wall
might look real,
but it's not
until the woman in the portrait
reaches out
of the gilt frame
to touch the vase
of anemones and ranunculus
that she remembers
how her fingers
once smelled truly floral—
not oil and turpentine,
not like dead plastic
trapped inside her
world, a shellacked
landscape
glossy as wax apples.

Steps Toward Healing

When you step waist-deep into a pond
and make yourself a ballerina tutu
from lotus blossoms, you'll dance
the pas de deux with settled sludge. And yet,
the pointed flower petals hold you up.
                    You won't drift.

You can lift your arms and leg in arabesque,
glissade back to shore, and leave wet tracks
among mint and marsh mallows. When you tell
your story, you won't leave out how
light you felt when buoyed, how
                    your valiant knight

bolstered you, fragile as an eggshell in a tempest,
small enough to fit into a lily of the valley bell.
Polish your ivory chevalier once again. You needn't
find him a new queen, needn't hold a magnifying
glass up to your eye
                    inspecting friends

or other mothers for your replacement.
You've learned to float on soap bubble gossamer,
how to fly the moon like a diamond kite, and how
to embrace brute jackals known as Warners,
Playtex, Maidenform without getting bitten.

Ancestry

I've borne the gears of the clock as they grind
beneath my petticoat, rib-scraped and listening
to the tick tock of that abrasion.

Maybe I should engrave the armor brass
which shuts this pocket watch? Tattoo
the scarred skin with magnolia buds?

But, Westminster chimes would still sound.
Someone's hand has set the mantel piece's pendulum.

*

I've read the bedtime fairytale to you, my child,
your blankets tucked against your chin,
and you've climbed the spiral staircase
foraging our garden in the dark.

Our home tree fills with cones & sticky needles,
and a raven has absconded with the housekey.
You ask, *Who ate the tarts?* and I can't say.

But, we'll hunt the brambles for the dragon
and its pet locusts lurking in our flower beds
until we slay them,
until the story reads "The End".

How many generations left to go?
I can't answer yet, my daughter, and to you
and to your sister, I can't apologize enough.

In the Pink Ribbon Parade

Violets follow the azaleas who follow
portulaca and poinsettia—who string together:
a long, unraveled yarn pulled from an old
sweater: good, crimped mohair.

Each face is a pinwheel flickering its story:
    pink and cobalt blurs into lavender
    the spokes of chariot wheels smudge as they circle

Each blossom is a note on the piper's sheet music
and rises toward middle C:
    the circus' calliope is distant
    dirges have been left unsung

Among this patchwork of calico quilt scraps,
I find my corner. I find my verdant page
in the storybook. Once its endpaper
was balled into a wrinkled scrum—a tumbleweed.
I smoothed it out.
Now, the whistle's blown to restart play.
The drum majorette lifts her hickory baton.

Peace

Beautiful things fill every vacancy
—C.D. Wright

Living underwater can shrivel a being, can
cause a mermaid to hug a fish-belly seahorse—
give up the palomino with the flowing mane.
She'll never catch the rainbow
trout unless she fashions a fishhook
from the barberry thorn and casts a slender
wisp of morning glory vine. It helps
to haul the iron anchor dropped to steady
a life raft or canoe
                    when there's only starting over.

A swan won't drown.
Her curved neck looks down at her reflection
in the still pond. She doesn't see the catfish
in the bottom mud. When under moonless dark,
her eyes blend in with the mirrored stars.

D. WALSH GILBERT is the author of *Ransom* and forthcoming in 2022, an all-ekphrastic poetry collection, *imagine the small bones* (Grayson Books).

A multiple Pushcart Prize nominee and winner of *The Ekphrastic Review*'s 2021 "Bird Watching" contest, her work has recently appeared in *Gleam, The Lumiere Review, Black Fox Literary Magazine, Riverbed Review, Peeking Cat Poetry,* and the anthology, *Waking Up to the Earth: Connecticut Poets in a Time of Global Climate Crisis,* among others.

She serves on the board of the non-profit, Riverwood Poetry Series, and as co-editor of *Connecticut River Review.*

Acknowledgements

Some images in these poems were inspired by the digital art of Catrin Welz-Stein: www.catrinwelzstein.blogspot.com. Thank you, Catrin, for contributing to this story.

Excerpts are included from *Alice's Adventures in Wonderland*, Lewis Carroll (England) 1865.

The author extends immense gratitude to the medical teams of Hartford Hospital in Hartford, Connecticut, USA, to the American Cancer Society, and the Reach to Recovery program.

The author would especially like to thank those people who consistently read her poems as they become poems, including her workshop groups: the PIPs and the Farmington Valley Chapter of the Connecticut Poetry Society. A huge thanks goes to Patricia Hale who generously read this collection first and to the good folks at *Cerasus Poetry* for publishing what took years for me to finally envision. Everyone together makes a good team.